'SOLA ADESAKIN

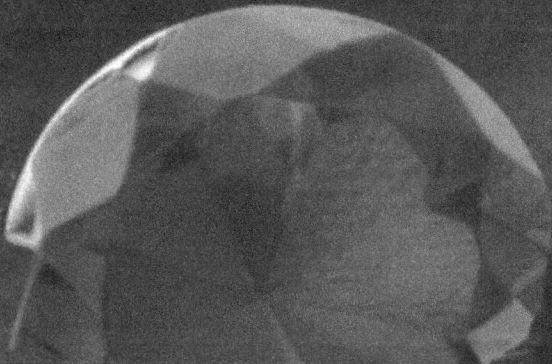

Rubies of Wisdom

40-DAY JOURNEY INTO FINANCIAL LIBERTY FOR EVERY WOMAN

Rubies of Wisdom
Copyright © 2016 by Sola Adesakin

Paperback ISBN: 978-978-955-758-5

Published by: FRUIT Foundation

Cover Design: Deji Akinpelu
Email: akintee79@yahoo.com

Printed in the United States of America.

CONTENTS

iii

TESTIMONIALS

There is a "how to go into the city"; Ecclesiastes 10:15.
"Rubies of Wisdom"- A compendium of wisdom is a breath of fresh air, a devotional with a difference. Highlighting the how to gain mastery and full of fresh perspective on the subject of finance, I believe strongly that this book will pass from generation to generation. It's a must read.

**Pastor Seun Uwubanmwen,
Deputy Pastor: His Treasure House Abuja, Nigeria**

"Rubies of Wisdom" is a relevant devotional for the 21st Century Christian woman who wants to be financial empowered and a responsible steward. Sola has done an extensive study on some women in the Bible with financial prowess. Some of the stories of these women in the Bible on the surface do not seem to have anything to do with money unless you look deeper like Sola has done. Thank you Sola for writing this thought provoking devotional and for shedding light on the delicate issues of managing finances. The lessons drawn out from each character's story is much needed today and I know will yield results when applied. I highly recommend this book!

'Detola Amure: Founder Super Working Mum: Author of Amazon Best Seller Super Working Mum, Living and Loving Life to the fullest. United Kingdom.

Just as the title says, "Rubies of Wisdom" is one devotional book filled with succinct words of wisdom from God's Word. Words that, when taken and practically applied to every area of your financial life, will catapult you from wherever you may be today to that mountaintop experience of abundance and prosperity in your finances. A book worth reading, and one in which Sola has generously shared her experiences, successes, and setbacks in dealing with finances with her readers, so that we also can take heed and learn. This is one book I absolutely recommend! –

Claire Abdul-Azeez Ogunbona: Medical Student & Freelancer, Ukraine.

"Rubies of Wisdom" is filled with wealth of wisdom and encouragement for women to rise, flourish and prosper. The 40-day devotional takes practical examples from the biblical women. In this devotional, my eye was particularly drawn to the Queen of Sheba who was educated, had the eagerness to learn, had the eye of an eagle and was ebullient. The characters that describe the Queen of Sheba are ones the women of today should mimic to get financial freedom. I have gained insight into biblical principles of wealth and financial freedom from this book. I will encourage all women especially wives and working mums to read this book. Well done Sola for this master piece. It is indeed going to change lives for financial freedom.

Mojisola Obazuaye: Image Consultant, Fashion and Inspiration Writer & Youtube Creator, Ireland.

"Rubies of Wisdom" is an awesome book. It is good to know that there are women who have done seemingly impossible things with their resources. This devotional is full of timeless lessons and experiences we can draw upon to put our finances in order and give our families the abundance experience"

Tosin Praise Fowowe: Family Finance Coach at Center for Sex Education and Family Life- Lagos, Nigeria.

"Rubies of Wisdom" is a beautiful reminder that we are not alone on the journey of becoming responsible financial stewards. Women of old as outlined in the Bible had similar struggles and through the grace of God prevailed - this grace has immense power!!! That same grace is available to us today to prosper and live in divine abundance as we live out the principles shared throughout this devotional. Thank you Sola for being a conduit of this message to our generation today as we embark on the journey towards financial freedom and the faithful stewardship of God's Heavenly resources here on Earth.

Lade Ayediran: Technology Vice President, Financial Services. New York.

My main take-away from "Rubies of Wisdom" is the first story; the widow with a debt profile that could only be cured if the creditor enslaved her sons. Anybody that is alive will incur expenses. A woman MUST have a means to settle these expenses whatever her pedigree. I learn from Sola on the Smart Stewards platform. She teaches us to monitor our finances so that we never experience what this woman had to deal with. Yes, miracles happen. God will bless and multiply what we own/have. Have more and His blessings will be on the 'more'. Sola, you are an inestimable gift to our world.

'Funke Fasunon: Virtual Lawyer (www.alpsedge.com); Wife & Mother to Her Main Business Partners- Lagos, Nigeria.

I am particularly excited about "Rubies of Wisdom" because it's full of wisdom from the scriptures. God has not left us guessing about any situation of life; there is an answer to every one of them in the Bible, our finances inclusive. Don't neglect the Bible in the pursuit of life, it's God's word to you and I. If you ever think your finances is important, then this book is a must read! So sit back and learn from the women of old! Just like 1 Corinthians 10: 11 says "All these things happened to them as examples; they were written down so that we could read about them and learn from them in these last days as the world nears its end" (paraphrased).

Gbonjubola Sanni: A Jesus Enthusiast, Accountant and Financial Literacy Advocate For Women and Children- Lagos, Nigeria.

I had goose bumps while reading "Rubies of Wisdom". It is so profound, insightful and extraordinarily remarkable. I am thrilled at the author's aptitude of expression and ability to unravel the wisdom in some of the female characters from both the new and Old Testament vis-a-vis today's Christian woman as it relates with her financial freedom and competence.
Each day of this devotional provokes your thinking and leaves you dealing with one of the Ds' mentioned; "date with greatness, dine with excellence and ditch mediocrity!" There is no better time to have a financial devotional for the Christian woman that points her to Jesus and His Word bringing out Gods best in her. It is a must read, get started!

Joy Yinusa: HRPB, Toronto Canada

vii

PREFACE

A lifetime of experience has birthed in me the burning passion to teach and encourage women along their journey to financial independence and freedom. Despite being a chartered accountant, I have had my fair share of struggles with money issues and sometimes still do. However I consider it a privilege, sharing some of my experiences coupled with money lessons from the women of the Bible in order to encourage women generally in becoming better money managers.

In this devotional, you will see the different dispositions and approaches the women of the Bible had toward financial and business issues, and how you can glean priceless insights from them. One thing is certain: women are natural nurturers who are quite able to multiply and effectively manage resources. However, a lot of us still struggle with the process of balancing personal lives, families, work and finances. We usually end up miserable as we find we are unable to effectively manage our God-given resources. As you embark on this 40-day journey with me, I sincerely hope and pray that within each day's study, you will quickly and easily identify the nuggets of financial wisdom therein. May you find the grace and strength to apply them for the change that you need. Amen.

Be Blessed!

With Love,

Sola Adesakin

ACKNOWLEDGMENTS

I am grateful to God for the inspiration and wisdom to write this book and for trusting me to be His voice in this generation and many to come.

A big shout out to all the members of Smart Stewards: a forum where I regularly teach on finance related issues. Thank you for believing in me.

To my ministry helpers at FRUIT Foundation, my sisters at Assisters, my mentees at S.A.G.E and my friends, family and loved ones all around the world, thank you for your support always.

I specially appreciate my Mentor; Pastor Nike Adeyemi for believing in my ability to talk on personal finance and the opportunity to have been featured on her "Real Woman With Nike Adeyemi" TV show that airs across the globe. Thank you Reverend Simeon Adenusi for your constant prayers and encouragement. I celebrate all my Mentors around the world.

I acknowledge and appreciate my husband Adegboyega for encouraging and supporting me to fulfill destiny; and our three (3) amazing sons; Babatamilore, Babafimidara and Babatitofunmi. I am incredibly blessed to have you as my family. I celebrate my Dad and Mum also.

Finally, thank you to Claire Abdul-Azeez Ogunbona, Ibinike Taiwo-Fajolu and 'Funke Fasunon for their efforts on this book.

INTRODUCTION

THINK M.O.N.E.Y

[14] *"For the kingdom of heaven is like a man traveling to a far country, who called his own servants and delivered his goods to them.* [15] *And to one he gave five talents, to another two, and to another one, to each according to his own ability; and immediately he went on a journey.*

Matthew 25:14

This biblical passage explains the mystery of stewardship. Everybody is endowed with: physical, financial, mental, and spiritual resources to manage. We will, in this book, be learning from different biblical stories how we can manage our resources better.

If you read the entire passage cited above, you will discover that when the master came back, the man who had gotten five (5) talents had traded with it and gotten five (5) more; same with the man who got two (2) talents, but the man who got just one (1) talent dug the ground and hid his talent; because he felt the master was being selfish by looking for returns where he never invested. Let us consider the talents as monetary talents.

The Stewards who are smart are future oriented; they have a managerial orientation, they think of generations to come, they think of giving accounts someday and have a dutiful disposition to deliver.

They are profit-driven....

The boss gave these three (3) men money to trade with; according to their capacity:

The first made double

The second made double.

The third did nothing other than to keep the talent.

The Rate on Investment (ROI) for the 1st two men was the same, despite the fact that the value of capital was different. The result was what mattered; not necessarily what amount they got as capital.

Sometime in the future, appraisals happened.

The result was anticipated

Those two got their promotion:

The third had lived for the present

He distrusted the boss, was concerned about his own immediate pleasure; lived a carefree life and was too lazy to work.

He failed woefully and he got a commensurate reward.

Every business owner is interested in his bottom line; He looks forward to getting returns. God is interested in His Investments in YOU.

Good money management entails a lot of principles such as Savings, Budgeting, Investments, Proper Planning, Earnings, Debt Management amongst others and in the course of this book, we will touch on each of these principles by highlighting them in the different bible stories.

Think Money, Think:

M: Managerial Mentality

O: Own your decisions and actions

N: Needs versus Wants- Evaluate thoroughly per time.

E: Earnings- Seek to increase it. Don't be lackadaisical.

Y: Yield - Make sure God's resources in your care are yielding something.

It's a New Day!

DAY ONE

❖

Planning For The Future.

(The Unnamed Widow At The Mercy Of Creditors)

"A certain woman of the wives of the sons of the prophets cried out to Elisha, saying, "Your servant my husband is dead, and you know that your servant feared the Lord. And the creditor is coming to take my two sons to be his slaves."
II Kings 4:1

A great place to start this devotional is with the unnamed widow whose husband had died and who had creditors threatening to take her two (2) sons as slaves for repayment. So let's do that!

Unfortunately, her husband, a committed man of God who was a son of the prophet Elisha, had died leaving a huge amount of debts behind for his wife, who was probably unemployed. Committed and God-loving but with no proper financial plan for his family, he had died with those debts unpaid. And here came the creditor threatening to take away his children as slaves. For whatever reason, he had failed to manage his finances well, so had his wife, and neither of them had anticipated his sudden death.

So this unnamed widow found herself and her children in a quandary; she had absolutely nothing to pay the creditor with. That is, until she came to the prophet Elisha who prophetically "rescued" her from the claws of the creditor. The lone jar of oil she had at home became the point of contact and an avenue into the newness of life. Thank God, she had something at least! Otherwise, the situation might have ended catastrophically for her family!

Every woman should have a backup plan for her family; as a support role to her husband if married. Whether you're a career woman or a stay-at-home mum, so long as you are there managing the finances of the family in one capacity or the other, it's financial wisdom to keep something aside for a rainy day. Miracles such as the one described above still happen, but wisdom dictates that nobody should consume all he/ she earns. "Precious treasure and oil are in a wise man's dwelling, but a foolish man devours it"- Proverbs 21:20

"A good person leaves an inheritance for their children's children, but a sinner's wealth is stored up for the righteous". Proverbs 13:22 (NIV)

Questions:

Do you have any debt as an individual or family?

How do you intend to pay them off?

Have you discussed a repayment plan with your debtors?

How can you increase your earning capacity?

Is there anything in your home that can earn you some more money?

DAY TWO

❖

Staying True to Your Vows.

(Hannah)

"Now when she had weaned him, she took him up with her, with three bulls, one ephah of flour, and a skin of wine, and brought him to the house of the Lord in Shiloh. And the child was young". I Samuel 1:24

Although this story does not relate that much to finances, there is a lot to be learned with regards to the vows we make, especially in dire moments. Many women in desperate situations make vows that they are unable to fulfill, intentionally or as a result of circumstances beyond their control.

Before you answer that altar call for a seed or pledge, settle it in your mind to pay your vow. It's better not to make a vow at all than to make and not fulfill it. One thing, however, is sure. God honors vows when they are fulfilled.

I have found myself struggling to pay up pledges in the past. Every time there was a call for pledges, I always felt pressured to respond. And sometimes, it would take years to pay some of them. No one should feel any undue pressure to respond every time a pledge is raised. Let God lead you and make sure you're convinced about it. God will only honor a pledge that comes from the heart. Not fulfilling your vow is inexcusable; the Bible is clear about that.

"When you make a vow to God, do not delay to pay it; For He has no pleasure in fools. Pay what you have vowed—Better not to vow than to vow and not pay".
Ecclesiastes 5:4, 5

At the right time, Hannah went up to pay her vow in the person of Samuel and with other items. It is recorded that she went with three bulls, an ephah of flour, and a skin of wine. This indicates to us that she was financially able to do this.

We can also conclude that Hannah, besides having five more children after paying her vow, also enjoyed the blessings of God immensely. Her heartfelt prayers in 1st Samuel 2:1-10 attest to this. This was because she had seen that God indeed lifts the beggar from the dunghill and the poor out of the dust!

"He raises up the poor from the dust; He lifts the needy from the ash heap to make them sit with princes and inherit a seat of honor". 1st Samuel 2:8

Questions:

Do you have any unpaid vows?

What plans do you have to pay them off?

What do you think is the reason for your inability to say no to calls for pledges/vows?

DAY THREE

❖

Building Lasting Wealth and Generosity.
(The Shunamite Woman)

"One day Elisha went to Shunem. And a well-to-do woman was there, Who urged
him to stay for a meal. So whenever he came by, he stopped there to eat. Let's make
a small room on the roof and put in it a bed and a table, a chair and a lamp for
him. Then he can stay there whenever he comes to us."
II Kings 4:8, 10 (NIV)

The story of the Shunammite woman is one of my favorites in the
Bible. It shows the life of a generous, God-fearing woman who had the
financial capacity to do what was on her heart.

It is important to say here that every woman should have something of
her own that generates some sort of income for her. That is one of the
essential keys to financial independence.

I will quickly mention that not everyone will be employed in a 9am to
5pm job. Some women will be homemakers, some employed outside
the home, others business-owners, and so on. I regularly advise women
that no matter how affluent their husbands or parents may be, or how
much has been bequeathed to them from their parents' estates, it is
always important to have something they can call their own.

Doing this gives a sense of fulfillment, a personal authority that none can gainsay, and the freeing flexibility to do what you want to when you want to. That's great because, as women, we usually have personal things we want to do; maybe that's to help the needy, or meet some other urgent need. The Shunammite woman was portrayed as an affluent woman.

Remember that her husband, who was quite old, had his thriving business too; it was recorded that their only son had developed an illness while he went to work with his father. Her husband had servants and donkeys (which are equivalent to modern-day exotic cars). Her husband may have empowered her, but she had some great things going on for her as well: she kept her business running smoothly while also effectively managing her home front. For that reason, she was able to suggest to her husband that they make a guest room and meals available for the itinerant prophet Elisha.

Frankly, it can be quite embarrassing for a woman to have to wait on her husband to meet her day-to-day needs; Sanitary towels, underwear, and all her petty needs. Sometimes, this becomes an area where division and animosity can set in.

Whenever I counsel women who feel offended that their husbands are not meeting their needs adequately, after calming them down, I usually ask how they met those needs on their own before getting married. Did they have to wait for a man to take care of little things like that?

Without trying to exonerate men who refuse to rise to their responsibilities, the truth is, life must continue!

I appreciate single ladies who enjoy their singlehood by making the best of their time without unnecessary excesses. Give yourself a treat from time to time without breaking the bank. Long gone are the days when a lady only looks forward to "enjoying life" after Prince Charming arrives. Be your own Princess Charming while you wait to tie the proverbial knot. Be good to yourself with all that God has blessed you with—within reasonable limits and a budget! I'm glad I was able to travel to several countries before I got married. Once you do get married, you'll come to find out that in marriage, your time and attention become divided.

That's especially true when you start to have children. Lady, have your own thing!

In the next devotional, I will share six amazing things you can identify in the life of the unnamed Shunammite woman.

"The hand of the diligent will rule, while the slothful will be put to forced labor".
Proverbs 12:24

Questions:

What plans have you put in place to become financially stable and strong or perhaps independent?

Can you balance your financial independence with a need to be provided for?

DAY FOUR

❖

Making Your Money Work For You.
(The Shunamite Woman)

*"Then Elisha spoke to the woman whose son he had restored to life, saying, "Arise
and go, you and your household, and stay wherever you can; for the Lord has called
for a famine, and furthermore, it will come upon the land for seven years." 2So the
woman arose and did according to the saying of the man of God, and she went with
her household and dwelt in the land of the Philistines seven years".*

*"So the king appointed a certain officer for her, saying, "Restore all that was hers,
and all the proceeds of the field from the day that she left the land until now."*

II Kings 8: 1-2, 8

Yesterday, we read about this prestigious woman, and in today's scripture,
we get a bit more insight into the depth of her wealth. She had fields and a
great household. She also got the proceeds from her field after she left the
country for seven years, all because Elisha spoke on her behalf!

In yesterday's devotional, we also discussed her hospitality and how
respected she was in the society. Today, we'll take the discussion a little
bit further. Though we may not know much about this great woman,
here are six Gs I see in her life.

Generous: She was a great woman, but that didn't stop her from helping

11

people. She provided a home and meals for Elisha, who was an itinerant pastor. Needless to say, she in return, had her needs met and was blessed with the fruit of the womb.

Gregarious: To be gregarious means to be friendly, amiable, and full of life. It doesn't matter what life serves on your plate. You should decide to turn lemons into lemonades and trust God to turn bitter waters into sweet springs. Serve your generation, be friendly, have a good disposition. Be known for good things, don't get weighed down by problems, be strong in the Lord!

Go-getter: In the bible days, there were only few women who were mentioned to have achieved or acquired so much as this woman had. She had fields, a large household as well; that must have required a lot of diligence and hardwork. She didn't have a child and dwelling on that could have hindered her from fulfilling other areas of purpose. God has blessed you and given you a vision, so go for it. Let no circumstance hinder you. Don't focus on what you don't have, rather focus on what and who you can become. You are more than you see today!

There are inspiring examples of women who have done amazing things. Mrs Ibukun Awosika comes to mind as I write this. She has recently been appointed as the First Woman Chairman of The First Bank of Nigeria and earlier on in her career, she established a furniture manufacturing company; a terrain that even men will cringe to go into. She is an example of a successful business magnate.

I admire Tara Fela-Durotoye; a pioneer in the bridal makeup profession in Nigeria. She has established a solid brand and has since trained so many ladies who are doing amazing things all over the world.

Gainfully occupied: More often than not, when someone is said to be wealthy, it is not just by wealth acquired or wealth transferred; wealth should also be measured by what you are able to accumulate by your efforts. This woman was introduced to us as wealthy; and we can see that she had her own source of wealth apart from what her husband had to give to her. The idle mind is the devil's workshop, they say. Keep yourself occupied, learn a skill, enroll for a course, start a charitable organization, help out in church. Continue to serve, and that great opportunity you desire will definitely come.

Grateful: A grateful heart is the springboard for a great life. If you are not grateful, you are a great fool, someone said. Keep your focus on the good things God has blessed you with. That is the secret of a happy and thankful heart. The Shunammite woman's grateful heart opened the door to more blessings in her life. Are you living a thankful life?

Godly: What a godly woman the Shunammite woman was. She held on to God, to His word and to His prophet in the face of challenges. Do you realize the popular phrase "It is well" that Christians (and practically everybody) use probably originated with her? It didn't matter what the circumstances looked like, she just kept saying "It is well!"

Questions:

Read the full story in 2nd Kings Chapter 4 and write down other godly attributes you see in this great woman.

Which of these attributes do you identify with?
What areas do you need to improve on?

DAY FIVE

❖

The Supportive Spouse.
(Priscilla)

"There he met a Jew named Aquila, a native of Pontus, Who had recently come from Italy with his wife Priscilla, because Claudius had ordered all Jews to leave Rome. Paul went to see them, and because he was a tent-maker as they were, he stayed and worked with them." Acts 18:2, 3 (NIV)

We have seen women who partner with their husbands in running businesses and who do very well. I once listened to Mrs. Odunola Oyegade, co-owner of Mopheth pharmacy, a leading pharmacy brand in Lagos, Nigeria about how their business started. At the meeting I attended, she shared her experience of starting her business with her husband over 18 years ago and how the business has grown by leaps and bounds.

It may be an uncommon occurrence for a woman to work in business with her husband. In fact, a lot of people might not support it: working with their husbands 9am to 5pm, and living with them for the remaining hours of the day, day in and day out! However, she proved it to be doable.

Our lady in focus from the Bible is Priscilla, who was a tent-maker just as her husband was. At some point in time, they hosted Paul the apostle, who was also a tent-maker. The tent-making business required a whole lot of skill and we can assume this woman was highly skilled. She ran the business with her husband, and it thrived. They were renowned not just as Christians, but also in the secular world, through their business.

You may not necessarily be in the same business line with your husband, but be ready to offer your assistance especially in areas you are skilled at e.g.; helping him with his business finance if you are an Accountant, lending your advice and expertise as an Architect if he needs to build.

I offer financial and business advice to friends, how much more my husband! I definitely will be compensated if not in cash, in kind and above all, his success is my success and the success of the entire family!

"He who finds a wife finds a good thing and obtains favor from the Lord".
Proverbs 18:22

Questions:

Do I have a place in supporting my husband's business?

If not physical support, how often do I pray for him?

DAY SIX

❖

Having it All Figured Out.
(The Virtuous Proverbs 31 Woman)
"Who can find a virtuous wife? For her worth is far above rubies.
11The heart of her husband safely trusts her;
So he will have no lack of gain. 12She does him good and not evil
All the days of her life.13She seeks wool and flax,
And willingly works with her hands. 14She is like the merchant
ships, She brings her food from afar.
15She also rises while it is yet night,
And provides food for her household,
And a portion for her maidservants". Proverbs 31:10-15

Women are natural nurturers. The description of the Proverbs 31 woman clearly highlights that. Married or unmarried, every woman should make it a responsibility to plan for her future family.

I understand the Bible says children should honor their parents, and that is definitely a must-do. However, parents should also endeavor to plan toward their means of livelihood especially in old age. These include retirement plans and dividend-yielding investments, among other things, so that they do not have to rely on what their children may or may not be able to give them.

16

It is the responsibility of parents, (the woman being the driving force, in my opinion) to secure the future of their children by giving them a good education, good investments and leaving good legacies for them. I am certainly not undermining the position of the fathers in this regard! They may be the one providing the financial resources, but the woman should strategically ensure these things are set in motion for a good and fulfilling future for the children.

Every Woman needs to be able to juggle roles first of all as an individual, a wife, a mother, a career person/business owner and a blessing to her world in general. None must work at the detriment of the other. The Proverbs 31 woman sets an example of someone who ensured the principle of work-life-balance was at play in her life. All areas adequately catered for. Proper planning is imperative for success in all these areas. Foresight is important too: paying bills at the right time; making yourself available at school meetings, being an achiever at work and at the same time, satisfying the needs of your spouse. The life of a woman seems to be a demanding one but I believe God adequately wired us to be multi-faceted and versatile.

It's amazing and inspiring that women are occupying a lot of roles that were prior to now occupied by men. Mrs Bola Adesola serves currently as the CEO of Standard Chartered Bank; Nigeria. A most worthy example is that of the Presidential Candidate of the Democratic Party in The United States; Hillary Rodham Clinton who is vying for the position of the President of The United States of America. If she wins, she becomes the first female president of America. Awesome!

Back to our point, a lot of times, there is pressure on us as parents to pay school fees. And, of course, the bills increase in geometric proportions as the children become older. Nowadays, it's amazing what crèches for infants and toddlers charge; not to talk of what one has to pay for high school and then for college or university! Wisdom dictates early planning.

Foresight teaches us that it is never too early to start saving up for a child, even before they are born. I have a friend who started saving for her unborn children while she was still expecting the fruit of the womb! I have opened banks accounts for each of my children. One for monthly savings from both my husband and I, and the other for gifts they receive from others. Maintaining these accounts requires a lot of self-discipline because sometimes, there's the temptation to quickly divert the monetary gifts to settle some pressing issues (can we be real here?) but accountability to God makes one do the right thing.

"The heart of her husband safely trusts her;
"So he will have no lack of gain. 12She does him good and not evil
all the days of her life". Proverbs 31:11-12

Questions:

How involved am I in my husband's and children day-to-day lives?

Are there investments I can make for my children now?

Is there a better way to manage the family finances in my custody?

When is the right time to start saving for the children?

DAY SEVEN

❖

Leaving Legacies for The Children
(Sarah The Mother Of All)

"Isaac brought her into the tent of his mother Sarah, and he married Rebekah. So she became his wife, and he loved her; and Isaac was comforted after his mother's death." Genesis 24:67 (NIV)

Sarah didn't have a child till she was ninety (90) and then she died at the age of one hundred and twenty seven (127). She was with Isaac for about thirty seven (37) years, but I am certain she made the best out of it. She had a tent, which Isaac chose to stay in when he got married. She left a befitting legacy behind for him, apart from what her husband had to give.

It is a good thing for your children to be wealthy and bless you, but it is honorable for you to also be a blessing to your children, their spouses and even grand children! By the grace of God, we trust that in this generation and subsequently, mother-in-law and daughter-in-law rifts will decline and eventually end (did I hear you say a big amen?).

In our generation and future ones, we will witness mothers-in-law being an immense blessing to their daughters-in-law; grandmas being a source of spiritual and material blessing e.g. buying exotic cars for their grandchildren and giving them gifts of houses! Our generation will experience it. You and I will see it happen through us in Jesus name! Like any mother would desire, I trust God that my children will be wealthy and do much more than we have done and will do, by the grace of God. And I trust Him also that I and my husband will continually be an immense source of financial and spiritual blessings to them as well.

Questions:

What legacies, spiritual and physical, am I passing on to my children?

Have you ever thought about your succession plan?

DAY EIGHT

❖

Paid To Raise Her Son: Trusting God To Take Care of Our Children.
(Jochebed)

"Then Pharaoh's daughter said to her, "Take this child away and nurse him for me, and I will give you your wages." So the woman took the child and nursed him".

Exodus 2:9

God orchestrated a plan that involved Jochebed getting paid to nurse her own biological son! God rewards and makes resources available for women somehow, some way! Those wages, I believe, were not meant to be spent on frivolous things. They were strictly for the upkeep and welfare of Jochebed as she took care of Moses and for Moses himself also. So be rest assured that God gives everyone the necessary resources to take care of their children; we are only co-partnering with Him after all. He is the One who owns them!

I particularly enjoy reading the story of Jochebed. She is such an inspiration to womanhood; a highly industrious and hands-on person. We didn't have so much to read about her husband Amram in the mystery surrounding Moses' birth but we see his mother, Jochebed, doing all she could to protect his destiny. I like the fact that she was able to design a basket that would float on the river without jeopardizing the life of the little baby. I wouldn't be surprised if the making and selling of Moses' baskets became Jochebed's trade!

Women by nature are excellent custodians and resource managers; that's who God made us to be! This leads me to my next point.

God, in His infinite mercies, will always make the necessary resources for nurturing our children available to us. Can you remember those times when your family experienced financial pressures and yet your children never lacked what they needed? Some of us went through school in spite of the hardships our parents encountered. That is the power of God at work. There's always provision when we co-partner with Him in raising our kids.

I know a lot of women who sometimes dip into their children's savings. We should be able to distinguish our children's funds from ours. Whenever they are given monetary gifts, save it up for them rather than spend it on family issues. Every woman must learn to save and also teach her children to do the same.

"Then God opened Hagar's eyes, and she saw a well full of water. She quickly filled her water container and gave the boy a drink.[20] And God was with the boy as he grew up in the wilderness. He became a skillful archer". Genesis 21:19 (NLT)

Questions:

How faithful am I with the resources I have to nurture my children with?

Am I giving them the best I can afford?

What effort am I making to raise contented children?

DAY NINE

❖ ————

*Building Great Things With our Hands: Power
To Build and Organize.*
(Jochebed)

*"So the woman conceived and bore a son. And when she saw that he was a
beautiful child, she hid him three months. But when she could no longer hide him,
she took an ark of bulrushes for him, daubed it with asphalt and pitch, put the
child in it, and laid it in the reeds by the river's bank".*
Exodus 2:2- 3

The Story of Jochebed is such an inspiring one that I can't but devote
another chapter to her. It is good to work for people but on the long
run, nothing brings fulfillment as much as what you build by yourself.
Every woman has the ability to build an empire. There are examples
around us of women who have risen through challenges of life and have
gone ahead to build legacies. Mrs Folorunsho Alakija ranked as the
wealthiest Black woman and her story is quite inspiring; so are Oprah
Winfrey's and Iman's and so many others that time will not permit me to
mention. You and I are on our way to building bigger things and the world
can't wait!

Some people, and their businesses, have become household names through
what they have been able to do with their hands. Many rake in billions

23

simply because of their skillfulness in using their hands. Consider professional makeup artistes, fashion designers, photographers, and many others. You too can achieve financial independence through the works of your hands.

For years, I believed that I didn't have any unique skill that could earn me money. I tried to learn how to sew, but that didn't turn into anything. I started to learn how to bake, but never finished, and so finally concluded I just wasn't a hands-on person.

Over time, however, I realized I was smart enough to organize things. I found I could design anything using my computer. I was computer savvy, and had the ability to study something new and put it to practice almost immediately. I could watch someone build a website and then replicate it myself! I wound up getting a whole lot of compliments in that regards, and then I concluded that, even though my giftings may not be in my hands, they were definitely in my brains!

Friend, it's about time you stopped complaining about your 9am to 5pm job not meeting your needs any longer. It's time for that introspective journey that will help you identify those things you can do either with your hands or with your brains! Those skills that will fetch you more money and lead you toward financial independence.

How I love women who can improvise, and create something big out of the insignificant; women who can reuse and recycle for the better. Jochebed, our focus in today's devotional, had to hide her baby in a basket. However, she also needed to make that basket as watertight and safe as possible, so the baby wouldn't drown in the river. Where was her husband?

24

He probably wasn't around to help and she also couldn't reach out to other men who may have helped her build the basket. Because that could have gotten her child killed!

And so she took uncommon things and created a lifesaver. That basket, which we now know as a Moses' basket, was worthy of being displayed in a museum! Mothers everywhere now purchase the Moses' basket for their newborns!

What you do with your hands can make you a household name long after you are gone. So, rise up, identify and put your gifts to use!

One more thing I like about Jochebed is the fact that she instilled good ideals into Miriam, who was her first-born child. The Bible expressly stated that Aaron was three years older than Moses, and scholars say Miriam was about seven years older. Therefore, we can deduce that when she had that conversation with Pharaoh's daughter, she was about ten (10) years old. Wow, I'll just leave the rest to your imagination!

Questions:

What are my God-given gifts or talents?

Am I using them adequately right now?

How can I translate them into money?

What am I teaching my children?

DAY TEN

❖

Averting Chaos By Tact And Wisdom.
Good Management of Resources(Abigael)

"Then Abigail made haste, and took two hundred loaves, and two bottles of wine, and five sheep ready dressed, and five measures of parched corn , and an hundred clusters of raisins, and two hundred cakes of figs, and laid them on asses. And she said unto her servants, Go on before me; behold, I come after you. But she told not her husband Nabal" I Samuel 25:18-19 KJV

Abigail is another woman I love to read about in the Bible. Not only is she described as a beautiful woman, but also as a woman who had "good understanding". Her husband, however, who was a very wealthy man, was described as churlish and wicked in his ways. We could assume that he satisfied Abigail's financial and material needs, but being the wicked and miserly man that the Bible describes, he might not have even been doing that! He certainly hadn't been willing to give any of his resources to David and his men. I strongly believe Abigail must have had her own source of income, which came in handy on the day of trouble.

A woman's tact, thriftiness and good management sense will always "preserve" her family in times of need.

Emergencies and Life are twins; they ride together. Every woman must be able to help her family put something in place to take care of

26

emergencies so that life does not come to a halt for the family. Emergency funds according to experts should be about 3-6 months worth of living expenses so that in case life happens; loss of income for example, the basic needs of the family are met. Between couples, the amount involved should be saved up and set aside.

"Charm is deceptive, and beauty does not last;
but a woman who fears the Lord will be greatly praised". Proverbs 31:30 (NLT)

It is a good thing to be endowed with beauty, but also in understanding and discretion! I like beautiful things, I like beautiful women; fanciful cars, nice houses and all; God has made all those things available for us to enjoy. It is a good thing for a man to enjoy the work of his lands and the fruit of his labour; but far more rewarding are the fruits of understanding wisdom, discretion. Wisdom is key in building a home; building legacies; in dealing profitably in businesses.

Question:

Do you have resources that can meet your needs should emergency arise?

DAY ELEVEN

❖
———————————— ◆ ————————————

The Power of Networking: Being Tactfully Adventurous.
(The Queen of Sheba)

"Now when the queen of Sheba heard of the fame of Solomon concerning the name of the Lord, she came to test him with hard questions. 2She came to Jerusalem with a very great retinue, with camels that bore spices, very much gold, and precious stones; and when she came to Solomon, she spoke with him about all that was in her heart. 3So Solomon answered all her questions; there was nothing so difficult for the king that he could not explain it to her".
4And when the queen of Sheba had seen all the wisdom of Solomon, the house that he had built, 5the food on his table, the seating of his servants, the service of his waiters and their apparel, his cupbearers, and his entryway by which he went up to the house of the Lord, there was no more spirit in her. I Kings 10:1-5

Every time I read the story of Solomon in the Bible, I am amazed by the extent to which a man can be loved, blessed and endowed by God. I greatly admire the character of Queen of Sheba who went to visit this blessed king.

She was one of the monarchs who reigned around the time of Solomon, and in today's (and tomorrow's) devotionals, I identify seven principles in her story, applicable to our modern-day businesses, careers and personal lives. The first four will portray her qualities, and the following three will show things she did for others.

1. **Educated**.

She likely had enough exposure herself, being a rich monarch, but she was willing to be more educated. She had heard of the fame of Solomon, the blessed of the Lord, and was more than willing to leave her land in order to see what his fame was all about.

This year, go out of your usual way of doing things. Aim to acquire more knowledge in your chosen field. Travel if you have to. Feed your eyes and mind with materials that will inspire you. Read wide, listen to the news, limit your watching of telenovenas and zeeworld, quit your followership of series and instead take online courses or attend seminars etc.

2. **Eagerness to learn.**

She didn't just come to view Solomon's wealth; she was willing to acquire knowledge from him as well. This was a lifetime opportunity for her. Many of us have the opportunity to mingle with highly successful people, but most of the time, we are carried away with the peripheral, like taking selfies with them! Only a few actually tap into the opportunity to learn from great men. Some are full of envy towards these personalities, and so can't even utilize such opportunity. No matter how much you've already achieved in life, determine to keep on learning! Enquire and seek to be educated. Wisdom can be acquired by learning and gleaning from those who have gone ahead in your career field. If you are into ministry, how have the older women done it and succeeded? Follow successful people, read their books, attend their conferences, buy their audio and video materials.

The dynamics of life is such that no man is born and grows up the same day; there is a learning process/curve and different phases for growth and development in life.

3. Eagle-eyed.

Within a short period after arriving, she was able to observe almost everything going on in Solomon's kingdom. She discussed with the king but at the same time, she observed everything: "the house he had built, the food on his table, the seating of his servants, the service of his waiters and their apparel and the appearance of his cup bearers".

I feel certain she went on to replicate those same things in her own kingdom.

When you see things that are beautiful and well-organized or maybe someone who does things excellently, what's your reaction? Do you learn from them, do you keep mental souvenirs from those experiences, and do you see things you can take back home with yourself and probably do better?

Be eagle-eyed. Nature clearly shows us the beautiful works of our God and we can, in addition, learn from others who have beautifully applied what God has endowed them with.

4. Ebullient.

To be ebullient according to the dictionary means to be "overflowing with fervor, enthusiasm or excitement". This queen came to the presence of the king enthusiastic. She eagerly looked forward to her trip, planned for it and truly, got more than she bargained for. Some encounters never leave you the same.

She saw so much that "there was no more spirit in her". Of course her spirit revived and she went back home more blessed.

In Proverbs 22:29, the Bible says that a man's gift will make him stand before kings. I'd also say a good disposition will make him heartily welcomed by the king. The queen wasn't haughty when she came to see King Solomon, in spite of her wealth. On the contrary, she was very eager to make good use of the opportunity and the king warmed up to her.

Questions:

What are you doing to improve yourself?

Which other ways can you better your chances of making that extra income or earning that position?

DAY TWELVE

❖

Learning from Others: The Power Of Warmth and Joviality.
(The Queen of Sheba)

In the previous devotional, I introduced us to the life of the Queen of Sheba; one of the most influential and richest monarchs who lived in the days of Solomon. She was rich enough to come visiting Solomon with massive gifts! Yesterday, we discussed four principles clearly evident in her life and in today's devotional, we will discuss three more.

5. **Endorse Others**.

Whenever you see something great in the lives of those around you, endorse, appreciate and acknowledge them. In doing so, your gifting will multiply and you will draw grace and wisdom as well.

The Queen of Sheba told Solomon that even though she had heard of his greatness, what she had seen with her eyes surpassed what she had been told. They were supposed to be contemporaries but she was not intimidated by his affluence and she freely acknowledged every good thing she saw!

"However I did not believe the words until I came and saw with my own eyes; and indeed the half was not told me. Your wisdom and prosperity exceed the fame of which I heard. 8Happy are your men and happy are these your servants, Who stand

continually before you and hear your wisdom! 9Blessed be the Lord your
God, Who delighted in you, setting you on the throne of Israel! Because the Lord has
loved Israel forever, therefore He made you king, to do justice and righteousness"
1st Kings 10: 7-9

6. **Exchange.**

O how I love this woman's wisdom! On her way to visit the wisest, richest and most endowed king of her time, she went with gifts. I wonder what gifts she could have gone with that he wouldn't already have a surplus of. Nonetheless, the Bible records that she arrived with a whole lot of gifts for the king. Let's have a look at some of what she gave.

"Then she gave the king 120 talents of gold, spices in great quantity, and precious
stones. There never again came such abundance of spices as the Queen of Sheba gave
to King Solomon." 1st Kings 10: 10-12

What a strong and wise woman she was!

The Bible records that, in return, she got all she desired from the king. She was noted for her generosity and there was nothing she asked the king for that she didn't get. Givers will always be rewarded.

Why don't you make this year your best year ever in terms of giving. Give to those who don't have, as a blessing to them, and also to those who do have. You will be greatly blessed in return.

7. **Enjoy**.

She arrived at Jerusalem with her retinue, had her desired audience with the king, observed everything she was able to, and most importantly, she enjoyed herself! She had a great time!

I'll encourage you to give yourself a treat from time to time. "Eat, Pray, Love", like a movie title says. Work hard and compensate yourself well. Enjoy and appreciate all that you have, no matter how little that may be at the moment. Enjoy life (with) your family, friendships, finances, career and everything God has blessed you with.

"Here is what I have seen: It is good and fitting for one to eat and drink, and to enjoy the good of all his labor in which he toils under the sun all the days of his life which God gives him; for it is his heritage.[19] As for every man to whom God has given riches and wealth, and given him power to eat of it, to receive his heritage and rejoice in his labor—this is the gift of God". Ecclesiastes 5:18-19

Questions:

Which of the principles discussed above is evident in your life and which of them will you like to imbibe?

How do you enjoy your leisure time?

Do you make time out to really give compliments and receive them?

DAY THIRTEEN

❖

Being Business Savvy.
(Lydia)

"Now a certain woman named Lydia heard us. She was a seller of purple from the city of Thyatira, who worshiped God". Acts 16:14

Some women's strengths are in buying and selling! I have friends and know of many others who have been in business all their post college/university lives; savvy business ladies, I call them.

Maybe it's just not my thing or maybe I'm just not just disciplined enough, but at all the different times I've ventured into buying and selling, I have never been able to sustain the business, even though I make good profits every time, from selling different things. This usually happens either because I am not able to follow up properly with collecting money from my clients, or from a lack of focus.

"Jack of all trades is master of none", as the saying goes. I have dabbled into shoe sales, clothes, gift items and so on.

Whenever I travel and find cheap items, I often buy with the intention of reselling them! While I usually do succeed in selling most of the items, I also end up giving a lot of it out for free! That doesn't make me a savvy business lady!

But I have realized how good I could be at doing many other things. I love to write and blog amongst many other things; I'd rather focus on those! Maybe buying and selling may become my thing in the future.

I have a friend who's never worked for anyone since she left school; she is an Entrepreneur to the core: make up artistry, bead making and shes doing very well!

Business requires discipline, focus, tenacity, and acumen. Carve a niche for yourself in your field of business, and follow through. You shouldn't go into a business because that's what's in vogue or because you think it might be profitable.

Back to our lady in focus; Lydia.

Now a certain woman named Lydia heard us. She was a seller of purple from the city of Thyatira, who worshiped God. The Lord opened her heart to heed the things spoken by Paul. And when she and her household were baptized, she begged us, saying, "If you have judged me to be faithful to the Lord, come to my house and stay." So she persuaded us. Acts 16:14, 15

The Message Bible says she was a "dealer in expensive textiles"; even back in those days! She created a niche for herself and was well known for it. She earned a place for herself in the Bible as well.

"Whatever your hand finds to do, do it with your might; for there is no work or device or knowledge or wisdom in the grave where you are going" Ecclesiastes 9:10

Questions:

What Business do I have a flair for?

What are my skills and areas of talents?

DAY FOURTEEN

❖

Achieving A Great Feat With Just A Small Cup.
Filling Your Pantry (Jael)

"Then he said to her, "Please give me a little water to drink, for I am thirsty." So she opened a jug of milk, gave him a drink, and covered him". Judges 4:19

A home should never run out of necessary supplies. That is a woman's responsibility. Even though I'm aware that sometimes the financial situation of the family could be a bit tight, I still believe it's the woman's responsibility to ensure that the basic needs of the home are in place. I find it totally unacceptable for a lady to have to go over to her neighbors to borrow a matchbox, soap, some measure of salt, and so on. I won't encourage it as an indulgence.

There's wisdom in making bulk purchases over a period of time. Proper planning will help you identify the items your family uses most frequently.

Groceries should be stored for certain periods of time; a month, quarter, etc. The more you use a grocery item, the more you can buy in bulk. Just imagine if Abraham and Sarah hadn't had anything on hand to offer the angels when they visited their home; they might have missed their visitation! How prepared are you to host a dignitary at the shortest notice?

I realized at one point, that because I lived in an area with easy access to supermarkets and shops, I was always running out of some basic thing or the other. Almost every night, I would ask my help to go buy something I urgently needed. Of course, it costs a lot more than buying in bulk and the stress of having to go out to pick petty items was just not worth it! I have coined Seven Fs for Personal Financial Management that I teach always and one of them is "Fill your Pantry Always".

The Israelites needed to get rid of their enemy and Jael's hospitality was what nailed it. Sisera, was commander of the Canaanite army of King Jabin of Hazor; the enemy of Israel at that time. And whilst the King of Israel had gone to war with Deborah; another powerful woman, Sisera found his way to Jael's house and needed to rest. The man asked for water but she gave him milk, thus getting him relaxed and then he slept off. Water on its own is refreshing, but the milk made sleep come more easily and thus, Jael was able to execute the enemy and oppressor of Israel. Her abode must have been quite clean and comfortable too! Trust God to meet all your family needs.

"The eyes of all look to you, and you give them their food in due season. You open your hand; you satisfy the desire of every living thing". Psalm 145:15-16

Questions:

How effective have you been in ensuring your family does not run out of basic supplies?

Can you entertain guests at short notice like Jael, Sarah, Cornelius' wife did?

DAY FIFTEEN

❖

Making Adequate Provision For The Children.
(The Mother Of The Boy With The Five Loaves
And Two Fish)

"There is a lad here who has five barley loaves and two small fish, but what are they
among so many?" John 6:9

So much has been said about the young lad who gave up his lunch box at Jesus' crusade, but very little about the woman, his mother I presume, who must have packed the lunch box for him.

She had prepared the meal with the intention of feeding her son, however, she also ended up feeding over five thousand (5000) men, not counting the women and children also fed. We can safely assume she must have gotten some; if not all the 12 baskets left over. May our supplies supply many and may they be multiplied in Jesus name. Amen.

On a different note entirely, an important part of financial fulfillment is being able to feed your family with good food and a balanced diet, rather than junk.

Many women, men, and even kids are now obese and I personally think the woman of the house; arguably is responsible for that to a large extent, besides other genetic causes. The internet has more than enough information on good feeding and dietary requirements for every stage of a child's development and for adults as well.

Across different continents and countries, there are usually particular foods that most people eat often. However, it's up to the woman of the house to help decide what's necessary and beneficial for the family.

Sometimes, finances may not be freely available, for example, in the case of the widow who only had enough flour and oil to prepare a final meal for her child. She eventually used them to prepare a meal for the prophet Elijah; she had something which God was able to multiply. May God multiply our little in Jesus name. Amen.

Simply put, there are five food groups everyone is meant to eat from and you can read up on that on the internet. Whatever we eat supplies our body with the necessary nutrients to support our health and daily activities. Daily intake should include Water, Protein, Fat and Carbohydrate, Vitamins and Minerals.

God fed the Israelites with Manna and Quails for many years and the bible recorded none was feeble among them. What He fed them with had all the necessary nutrients for survival.

Question:

Am I deliberate and conscientious about what I feed my family with?

DAY SIXTEEN

❖

Co-ordinatng Events At Short Notice.
(Esther)

"So Esther answered, "If it pleases the king, let the king and Haman come today to the banquet that I have prepared for him." 8If I have found favor in the sight of the king, and if it pleases the king to grant my petition and fulfill my request, then let the king and Haman come to the banquet which I will prepare for them, and tomorrow I will do as the king has said." Esther 5:4, 8

Similar to one of our previous devotionals, in which we discussed the ability to put things together within a short period of time, I'd like us to take a look at the life of Queen Esther and how she was able to get independence, even though not financial, for the entire nation of Israel.

It is arguable that being the queen gave Esther all she needed to put a banquet together for two consecutive days. However, we must assume that she must also have been deeply involved in ensuring that all was perfectly arranged and organized.

Her husband, the king, was a very fussy person; rich, a party lover (Remember his first wife, queen Vashti, had been removed because of her refusal to display herself before him and his subjects in their drunken state at an earlier party/banquet).

King Ahasuerus was a carefree person, who loved fun and pleasure, and I suspect he would have had a high taste when it came to things of affluence.

Esther needed a favor from him and God gave her strategy for getting it. She was to get through to the king using that which he enjoyed most; banquets and partying. She had fasted and prayed, and adequate preparation for the banquet was all that was left to nail her divine plan.

It is important to note also that for Esther to have been able to put all these together, she had her own provision. She didn't have to wait on the king for provisions or sustenance. If it had been so, she might not have been able to successfully execute her plans of hosting the king for two consecutive days. My highly revered Mentor and Matriarch of Faith; Reverend Funke Felix-Adejumo, emphasized in one of her sermons I listened to, the importance of a woman having "her own thing" using Esther as an example. When you have your own thing, you can take apt decisions which would be in the interest of the family as well.

The ability to organize is a necessary skill for getting the best out of life, especially for a woman who wants to be financially independent. You must be able to articulate your plans and execute them, especially when an opportunity comes up at short notice.

It may not be easy to get one's plan in order one hundred percent of the time but it's always better to plan a little than not to plan at all. Failure comes as a result of improper planning. And planning is necessary for every facet of life.

Usually, whenever I go on vacation, before leaving, I draw up a schedule of where I plan to be and when. I do my best to schedule everything in an organized manner. Details like how long I'll be staying at a particular place, when I'll be getting there, and so on and it makes life a whole lot easier!

Despite all that though, I make sure to never forget that popular saying –man proposes, and God disposes! I make sure never to leave out the God factor!

"So the king and Haman went to dine with Queen Esther. And on the second day, at the banquet of wine, the king again said to Esther, "What is your petition, Queen Esther? It shall be granted you". Esther 7:1-2

Questions:

What kind of hostess are you?

Can you family rely on you to put up with last minute orders without breaking the bank?

DAY SEVENTEEN

Hospitable Enough to Entertain Even Strangers.

Understanding Your Own Area Of Strength (Martha)

———————— ❖ ————————

"Now it happened as they went that He entered a certain village; and a certain woman named Martha welcomed Him into her house. 40But Martha was distracted with much serving, and she approached Him and said, "Lord, do You not care that my sister has left me to serve alone? Therefore tell her to help me."
Luke 10:38, 40

I remember writing an article titled "Mary's heart, Martha's Hands". We can observe that Jesus must have been quite close to them, since he was going to have lunch in their home. On getting there, He immediately began to teach while waiting for the meal; as usual, never losing priority focus on what God had sent Him to do. Of course, someone had to get the meal ready and here, we see Martha playing the perfect hostess.

That must have been her core area, what she loved doing; organizing things, setting up for events, catering, and so on. She may have had a knack for doing all of those things and ensuring everything was hunky dory. And so, while Jesus was teaching with Mary at His feet, aptly learning, Martha was all over the house, putting everything in place to make the Master physically comfortable.

Eventually, however, she couldn't hide her disgust when her sister refused to lend a helping hand and she blurted out in anger asking why Jesus would allow her sister to sit at His feet, while she was doing all the work, cooking and setting the table.

We could easily conclude that Martha was the outgoing one. On the other hand, we see a more introverted Mary whose priority appeared to be feeding on the Word and building herself up spiritually. She seemed less of a hands-on person, and more of an intellectual and introvert.

Martha ministered to the Savior's physical needs by providing food for Him. Needless to say, hearty meals were important for this itinerant teacher and preacher. Even though Jesus was and is the Savior of the world, He came as a human, and experienced hunger just like we do. He had a need for food just like you and I do. Mark 11 verse 12 says Jesus was hungry.

So Martha ministered to that area of Jesus' life whenever he was with them because that was her area of gifting. However, Mary connected with Him on another level entirely; she served in worship and learning at the Master's feet. Give it to both of them, they were sisters but differently wired.

There's no point in making unhealthy comparisons, no point trying to run another man's race. The Master created you, wired you up, knew you before you were ever conceived, and He loves you just as you are! He isn't partial, and He doesn't play favorites. He reckons with you based on the giftings he has put in you.

Just as the car is made to be driven on the road, the ship to sail on water, and planes to fly, God doesn't expect you, as a car, to fly or a plane to sail on water! Martha was action-oriented and active, while Mary was gentle and introspective.

Martha had gifted hands to help but Mary had an intellectually sound and receptive mind. Whatever capacity you've been assigned to serve in, whatever your giftings may be, and whatever God is doing through you, be glad for them! If you're called to preach, do it heartily; to sing, do it with joy; to clean the toilets in church, wear a beautiful smile as you go about it.

As you stay in your calling, you will definitely be celebrated. You are special and what you do is beautiful in His sight. Quit the comparison game. Sure, you can be inspired by what others do, but don't become envious of them or try to pull them down. It is unwise to envy and backbite people who are successful, forgetting that they must have paid their dues for success. Funke Akindele has revolutionized comic acting in Nigeria and you see a lot of young girls aspiring to be like her.

Friend, it's time for you to be celebrated. Love yourself just as the Master loves you, and enjoy your giftings. Whether it's Martha's hand, or a Mary's mind; a conspicuous ministry or a less obvious one; always give your best!

"As each one has received a gift, minister it to one another, as good stewards of the manifold grace of God". I Peter 4:10

Question:

Am I optimally using my gifts and talents without feeling insecure with regards to other peoples accomplishments?

DAY EIGHTEEN

❖

Being A Blessing To Your Mother/Mentor.
(Ruth)

"So she gleaned in the field until evening, and beat out what she had gleaned, and it was about an ephah of barley. Then she took it up and went into the city, and her mother-in-law saw what she had gleaned. So she brought out and gave to her what she had kept back after she had been satisfied". Ruth 2:17-18

Being a mother myself, I must say kudos to mothers time and time again. The entire process of conceiving, birthing, nurturing, and finally releasing a child to his/her destiny is no joke. Mothers sacrifice a whole lot, and so do spiritual mothers who nurture spiritually by providing guidance, direction, and support to their spiritual children.

We all have a responsibility to be a blessing in return to our biological and spiritual mothers/parents. In my native dialect, Ruth from the Bible is referred to in a proverb, where she is described as a woman who was overly clingy to her husband... But, wait a minute, it was actually Naomi, her mother-in-law and not her husband, that she had refused to let go of. Her husband was already dead.

She saw good virtues in Naomi's life and she refused to let go. Even when she began to enjoy more of God's blessings, she did not forget her mentor.

I have realized from experience the importance of mentoring. I thank God for blessing me with Good Mentors. Earlier this year, February 2016 to be precise, I got a message from My Mentor, Pastor Nike Adeyemi that she would be having me as a guest on her TV show that airs around the globe to talk alongside with her about Financial Wisdom. And I remember her saying "I believe in you". Wow! I have never been on TV; I was not considering going on TV at that time, I was just doing my thing, teaching about personal finance in my corner(as I still do), but I believe she saw that I had something to offer and she invited me. It was such a humbling and awesome experience for me. I will be forever grateful to her and God for it. Talk about the power of mentoring. Mentors bring out the best in people and they deserve to be recognized and celebrated.

Have you noticed that when Ruth gave birth to Obed, the women of the town celebrated Naomi? And not only that, she was the one who cared for the baby. The women said *"Now at last, Naomi has a son again"* (Ruth 4:14-17). Ruth could credit and trust her achievements to Naomi; because she deserved it. So Ruth got her rewards and shared her blessing with her mother and mentor.

"And we urge you, brethren, to recognize those who labor among you, and are over you in the Lord and admonish you, ¹³ *and to esteem them very highly in love for their work's sake".* 1st Thessalonians 5:12-13

Questions:

Who are those who have labored over me to ensure I succeed?

How can I be a source of blessing to them?

DAY NINETEEN

❖

Giving Financially To The Service of God.
The Importance Of Giving:(Joanna and Mary Magdalene)

"And certain women who had been healed of evil spirits and infirmities—Mary called Magdalene, out of whom had come seven demons, and Joanna the wife of Chuza, Herod's steward, and Susanna, and many others who provided for Him from their substance". Luke 8:2-3

There is nothing so rewarding and fulfilling as giving to the Lord. A giving woman is a winning woman. I have personally enjoyed the benefits of giving my time and money to God, and I have both seen and heard testimonies of bountiful results from those whom God greatly blessed as a result of their giving attitude; whether it was giving to God's work or giving to the poor. I can't even explain this enough.

The women mentioned above- Mary Magdalene, Joanna and Susannah were women who gave extensively to the ministry of Jesus when He was on earth. The Bible records that they gave "from their substance", thus placing further emphasis on the fact that a woman must have "substance". One might argue that Joanna had substance because she was married to King Herod's steward; but it was still hers.
The Bible did not indicate Susannah's marital status, but we know for sure that Mary Magdalene was not married. Yet she was a giver.

The business of giving is not reserved only for the married women. In fact, I believe single ladies are in a more privileged position to give, because, most often, their only accountability is to the Lord. They have all of their resources are at their sole disposal and can do with it as they please, without the need for approval from their husbands.

Don't get me wrong. Marriage does not mean you can't spend your money as you wish, but the truth is; in marriage, "the two become one", and so decisions have to be agreed upon by both husband and wife. Even if not for the purpose of obtaining permission from her husband, a wife may still have to inform him of her financial decisions.

"Give, and it shall be given unto you, good measure, pressed down, shaken together, and running over" (Luke 6:38). Giving to God and humanity out of our substance should be a lifestyle. There's so much joy in sharing with those who are in need and being a blessing in our local churches; especially when needs arise. I have walked in that grace but I desire more of it. It's very rewarding. It's a beautiful thing to be a giver. It feels fulfilling when you are able to put a smile on someone's face and, besides that, the rewards could be overwhelming. Many times, your own needs are met in amazing ways. God also makes a way for you and opens doors in unexpected ways.

"And let our people also learn to maintain good works, to meet urgent needs, that they may not be unfruitful". Titus 3:14

Question:
In what way can I be a blessing to projects in my local assembly as well as meet the needs of others?

DAY TWENTY

❖

Partnering With God For Good Works. The Importance of Good Work Ethics: (Puah And Shiphrah)

"Then the king of Egypt spoke to the Hebrew midwives, of whom the name of one was Shiphrah and the name of the other Puah;

17But the midwives feared God, and did not do as the king of Egypt commanded them, but saved the male children alive.

20Therefore God dealt well with the midwives, and the people multiplied and grew very mighty". Exodus 1:15, 17, 20

As career-women, we can help to propagate goodness. Puah and Shiphrah feared the Lord and gave their allegiance to God, by "helping" the people of God. Pharaoh, a wicked king, had instructed both midwives to keep the baby girls they delivered alive and kill the boys.

What do you mean, kill? Strangle them once they're born, or what? Throw them in Nile, I think!

Puah and Shiphrah; the Hebrew midwives who worked in the secular Egyptian palace, partnered with God to be life preservers and not life takers. They chose to fear God instead, and found a way around the instruction, knowing they could have been killed for it!

What was their reward? God honored them and multiplied them. He gave them households of their own! God never leaves a giver empty-handed.

At work and wherever we find ourselves, we should stand for what is true and right even when it seems our job security is threatened. Be God's eye, God's Partner in the midst of a crooked world.

"For God is not unjust to forget your work and labor of love which you have shown toward His name, in that you have ministered to the saints, and do minister".
Hebrews 6:10

Question:

How can I be a source of blessing right at my place of work and how can I partner with God for the good of others?

DAY TWENTY ONE

❖

Being a Sacrificial Giver
(The Woman With The Alabaster Box)

"There they made Him a supper; and Martha served, but Lazarus was one of those who sat at the table with Him. Then Mary took a pound of very costly oil of spikenard, anointed the feet of Jesus, and wiped His feet with her hair. And the house was filled with the fragrance of the oil". John 12:2- 3

Mary did something so significant that it landed her an eternal recognition in the Bible. She broke a box of oil, which could have been sold for a lot of money, and anointed Jesus' feet with it. She did not only anoint Jesus but her action affected the entire house and its occupants as the entire area was filled with the fragrance from the oil.

The oil was an expensive one and it must have cost a fortune, but Mary knew all that mattered was giving her best to her Master, Her loving Teacher. She may not have been able to cook, but she sure knew what to do to touch the Savior's heart and that she did. However, we again see Martha doing what she knew best: serving.

"But one of His disciples, Judas Iscariot, Simon's son, who would betray Him, said, 5 "Why was this fragrant oil not sold for three hundred denarii and given to the poor?"

6 This he said, not that he cared for the poor, but because he was a thief, and had the money box; and he used to take what was put in it. 7 But Jesus said, "Let her alone; she has kept this for the day of My burial. 8 For the poor you have with you always, but Me you do not have always." John 12:4-8

Mary had spiritual insight when she anointed Jesus with oil, and we later see that her actions and gesture were prophetic as Jesus pointed out in the subsequent verses. The spiritual purpose of her actions had been to prepare Him for his burial!

On the other hand, there's the unnamed woman in the Bible who poured an expensive, full jar of alabaster oil over Jesus' head. Jesus had gone visiting Simon, one of His followers who had benefited from His ministry and this woman had found her way there probably uninvited. She hadn't come to touch the hem of His garment, neither had she come to make a request. She simply wanted to pour out her love on the Master.

This woman poured oil on Jesus' head and it must have been dripping down his face and clothes. That must have taken a lot of courage but she didn't care! She was driven by something much deeper than the superficial. (Matthew 26:7).

Many times, we only want to receive from God and from others, forgetting that "it is more blessed to give than to receive", as the Bible admonishes. Our world is hurting today because of a lack of genuine love and compassion among men. Why would someone rape another person? Why would a man assassinate another man? Why is there contention and war among members of the same household? Why is there hatred and envy among mankind? Simply because love is lacking!

Some of the people there became angry and said to one another, "What was the use of wasting the perfume? It could have been sold for more than three hundred silver coins and the money given to the poor!" And they criticized her harshly.

Mark 14:4, 5 (GNT)

The guests at this table where Jesus sat felt that this woman should simply have sold the expensive alabaster oil and given the money to the poor. However, Jesus made them realize that her act of anointing Him with the oil had been birthed out of love and not just giving!

Let's look at it from another angle: sometimes people may criticize you for being an "extremist" in the service of God: your visits to orphanages; helping the poor; and so on. They get angry with you like they got angry with this woman. The Bible said that they criticized her harshly! She had something that they didn't, and the Savior was not embarrassed by the fact that His clothes and body must have been messed up by the oil. It was coming from a heart of love! She took an expensive oil and poured it over Jesus' head–she gave her all.

Others criticized her, but Jesus appreciated her gesture.

Generations will remember you for your genuine, heartfelt service to God and man. Never relent! Givers never lack!

"Assuredly, I say to you, wherever this gospel is preached in the whole world, what this woman has done will also be told as a memorial to her" Mark 14:4

Question:

Do I possess anything I won't be willing to give to the Lord if He requires it?

DAY TWENTY TWO

❖

Courage To Request For What's Rightfully Yours.
(Daughters Of Zelophehad)

"Zelophehad son of Hepher had no sons; he had only daughters, whose names were
Mahlah, Noah, Hoglah, Milkah and Tirzah.) And they stood before Moses,
before Eleazar the priest, and before the leaders and all the congregation, by the
doorway of the tabernacle of meeting, saying: 3 "Our father died in the wilderness;
but he was not in the company of those Who gathered together against the Lord, in
company with Korah, but he died in his own sin; and he had no sons. 4Why should
the name of our father be removed from among his family because he had no son?
Give us a possession among our father's brothers." Numbers 27:2-4

The woman who will be financially free is the woman who will demand for her rights in life. Life is like a vast ocean with lots of fish. You could walk on the seashore, or ride boats through the waters, but if you don't throw your nets into the water, you'll never catch any fish!

It's not enough to know that there are many different species of fish in the water; you have to take action and go fishing to get what you want. More so, failing to catch anything at some point does not mean you should stop trying!

These four unmarried women took the bull by the horn. They argued that if they were not allowed to inherit, then their father; Zelophehad's name would be lost to his clan. The situation was that their father was dead and he had left behind an inheritance. They likely didn't have any basis to talk or express their opinions, but they had the courage, and God spoke for them. Thus, a rule was established because of their courageous act.

Life will deliver to you only that which you demand from it. Press on in the field of business; it's way too early to give up. Especially in the days of little beginnings, when it seems nothing is happening.

Submit and resubmit your proposals, your resume, and don't be afraid to ask over and over again. There's power in persistence and double power when it's accompanied by patience.

Always be willing to also assist others in their journey. That's a key source of blessings. Whenever you help others, God helps you too.

"For God has not given us a spirit of fear, but of power and of love and of a sound mind". 2nd Timothy 1:7

Question:

Are there God-inspired steps I am hesitating to take?

DAY TWENTY THREE

---❖---

The Importance Of Sound Moral Decisions and Teaching Them To Children.

(Micah's Mother)

"Now there was a man from the mountains of Ephraim, whose name was Micah. 2And he said to his mother, "The eleven hundred shekels of silver that were taken from you, and on which you put a curse, even saying it in my ears—here is the silver with me; I took it." And his mother said, "May you be blessed by the Lord, my son!" He returned the money to her, and she said, "I now dedicate these silver coins to the lord. In honor of my son, I will have an image carved and an idol cast." 4So when he returned the money to his mother, she took 200 silver coins and gave them to a silversmith, who made them into an image and an idol. And these were placed in Micah's house".

Judges 17: 1-4

The lessons we can learn from this story are many. We see the chapter starting off with Micah, who returned the shekels of silver he had stolen from his mum. He did that because he heard her place a curse on the thief.

Now our focal point in this story is what his mum went on to do with the shekels in "honor" of her son. This was a period in time when the Isrealites were being regularly admonished by God through His prophets to draw closer to God and forsake idol worship. But here was this mother from the tribe of Ephraim, paying a silversmith for an idolatrous image for her son. You'll also notice that she never even rebuked him for the theft.

Many women nowadays purchase "idols" for their children in the name of love and pampering. Children should certainly be loved, but they should also be taught and corrected. Let's never pass on things that don't glorify God to them. We should never succumb to their whims and caprices. Teach them accountability, teach them savings, teach them how to manage their finances, teach them respect.

"Train up a child in the way he should go, And when he is old he will not depart from it". Proverbs 22:6

Questions:

Do I succumb to the whims and caprices of my children?

Do I give them what they want or what they need?

Do I correct them whenever necessary?

How can I ensure I don't turn my children to mini-gods?

DAY TWENTY FOUR

❖

The Pitfall Of Enjoying Inappropriate Returns.
Discerning Ungodly Gains (Sisera's Mother)

"From the window Sisera's mother looked out.
Through the window she watched for his return, saying,

Why is his chariot so long in coming? Why don't we hear the sound of chariot
wheels?'29 "Her wise women answer, and she repeats these words to herself:

30' They must be dividing the captured plunder—with a woman or two for
every man. There will be colorful robes for Sisera, and colorful, embroidered
robes for me. Yes, the plunder will include colorful robes embroidered on both
sides." Judges 5:28-30

Sisera's story is not entirely new in this devotional. Remember he been
killed by a "stay-at-home mum" called Jael (see Day 14). It's obvious to
us from the verses above that Sisera's mother was used to her son
bringing back spoils of terror. Sisera had been a terror to the Israelites
and had regularly harassed, oppressed, and exploited other nations.

Every woman wants to be financially comfortable, and pampered by her
children, especially when they start working. That would be some sort of
compensation for years of laboring over that child. It is, however, sad that
some mothers don't even know the source of their children's wealth.

I once heard a popular story about an armed robber who, moments before being executed for his crimes, beckoned to his mum to come closer to him so he could whisper a word to her. On moving closer to him however, he instead bit her on the ear, and then accused her of having enjoyed his stolen goods without ever discouraging him from the thefts!

In our quest for comfort for and from our children, let's always ensure they do what's right and acceptable!

"The rod and rebuke give wisdom, but a child left to himself brings shame to his mother". Proverbs 29:15

Question:

Do I allow my children continue in unacceptable practices?

DAY TWENTY FIVE

❖

Determination In The Face Of Adversity.

(Achsah)

"And Caleb said, "He who attacks Kirjath Sepher and takes it, to him I will give Achsah my daughter as wife." 17 So Othniel the son of Kenaz, the brother of Caleb, took it; and he gave him Achsah his daughter as wife". Joshua 15:16-17

Imagine getting home from school on a sunny afternoon, after a hard day's work attending lectures and presentations on your journey to becoming a medical doctor with no thoughts of marriage on your mind, You see a couple of cars at the entrance of your house.

"Is anything the matter Dad?"

"Hmm... No, only that I got into a business agreement and my part of the deal is to give you out in marriage to this man, and he is here to take you to a remote town thousands of mile away..."

Achsah, Caleb's daughter, happened to find herself in a similar situation. Her father had vowed to "give her as wife" to anyone who successfully attacked and captured the land of Kirjath Sepher. Othniel the son of Kenaz did so, and here he was with his family and friends, to claim his prize!

Life can be funny and unpredictable with its many twists and turns. Here, we have a lot to learn from the story of a young girl who was bold enough to turn life's lemons into lemonade. Having been wedded off, most likely without her consent, her hopes shattered and aspirations truncated, she remained determined that her best days were still ahead of her.

You can read the full story in Joshua 15:16 and Judges 1:12, where it was recorded word-for-word twice! What amazes me about Achsah was her steadfast determination to get the best out of life. She had life going on pretty well for her, I'm guessing, and all of a sudden, she was being "given out free of charge" to some man!

"Now it was so, when she came to him, that she persuaded him to ask her father for a field. So she dismounted from her donkey, and Caleb said to her, "What do you wish?"
19 She answered, "Give me a blessing; since you have given me land in the South, give me also springs of water." So he gave her the upper springs and the lower springs"
Joshua 15:18-19

"Give me a blessing, give me springs of water", she demanded from her father. She also urged her husband to ask for a field from her father. She was wise enough to prepare herself and her posterity for the future. She felt no need to embrace bitterness or court excuses!

I recently read the story of Winifred Selby; a Ghanaian National who at fifteen (15), co-founded the Ghana Bamboo Bikes; an organization that specializes in building bikes made of bamboo and suitable for high terrain and rough roads. It is recorded that her family struggled with

64

finances and she had to sell toffees and small things to assist her family. Now twenty (20) years old, she is an inspiration to aspiring entrepreneurs around Africa and her story has been featured by the likes of Forbes, Elle and she has also hosted a TEDtalk with TEDx Accra.

I'll like to list out just seven Ds for you to think about.

1. Discover yourself–Identify your gifts

2. Be Determined–Barriers notwithstanding

3. Be Diligent–Give yourself wholly to what all that you do

4. Be Dedicated–Learn all you need to. Be passionate

5. Be Disciplined–Curb your excesses

6. Diversify–Identify other opportunities in your life

7. Date greatness, dine with excellence, and ditch mediocrity!

"Be anxious for nothing, but in everything by prayer and supplication with thanksgiving let your requests be made known to God". Philippians 4:6

Question:

Which of the Ds listed above do I currently lack?

DAY TWENTY SIX

❖

The Benefits of Multitasking: The Power Of Excellence.
(The Proverbs 31 Virtuous Woman)
"She girds herself with strength,
And strengthens her arms.
18She perceives that her merchandise is good,
And her lamp does not go out by night.
19She stretches out her hands to the distaff, And her hand holds the spindle.
20She extends her hand to the poor, Yes, she reaches out her
hands to the needy.
21She is not afraid of snow for her household,
For all her household is clothed with scarlet.
22She makes tapestry for herself;
Her clothing is fine linen and purple". Proverbs 31: 17-22

Diversify: Everyone has at least one gift, and the potential to multitask.
The first man God created could tend the flock, care for the plants,
nurture the garden, assign names to God's creation and more. That's a
prototype of what men (and women) can be.

In a world of ever-increasing costs, every woman has to consider
increasing her income. How can we increase our income if we're stuck
in one job, especially when salary increases and promotions come only

once a year (or never at all)? In many offices, promotions don't even visit in years.

In seeking multiple income streams, there are a number of things to consider:

Your strengths (some are born talkers, others motivators, and others writers);

What you enjoy doing (some love to travel a lot); you'd be shocked at the businesses that can come out of that.

So how can these translate into money for you? Simply go for it, start somewhere! Many people start with the things they love doing. What you love is a stepping stone to what people will love you to do for them.

Above all, be passionate about life, your gifts, talents, and just as importantly, the people you are serving. This will help you give your best, and they'll keep coming back for more.

"Whatever your hand finds to do, do it with your might; for there is no work or device or knowledge or wisdom in the grave where you are going".
Ecclesiastes 9:10

Questions:

What gifts and talents do I have?

How can I turn my passions to profit?

DAY TWENTY SEVEN

—————————— ❖ ——————————

The Danger Of Opposing The Needy With One's Resources.
Collaboration Is Key (Peninnah)

And her rival also provoked her severely, to make her miserable, because the Lord had
closed her womb. 7 So it was, year by year, when she went up to the house of the Lord,
that she provoked her; therefore she wept and did not eat. I Sam 1:6-7

Peninnah can be likened to that modern-day woman who has a lot of possessions and poorly treats those who don't have as much as she has. A Peninnah will look down on you at the slightest opportunity, just because you have a need or you don't seem to measure up to her in society.

She delights in provoking others for no good reason. Even if you have good reason to get back at your neighbor for a wrongdoing, it is best left for God to handle.

A Peninnah is a proud woman who has no regard for authority or for those who are ahead of her in life, and can talk to anyone rudely. The Bible listed Hannah as the first, and Peninnah as the second wife, so Hannah was most likely the older wife; in terms of age and even in marriage.

It was apparent Elkanah loved Hannah and if Peninnah had respected him, shouldn't she also have shown some amount of respect for Hannah as well? Maybe Elkannah had caved in at some point to the pressure of marrying another wife, since his first wife was not bearing children. The decision might have been a difficult one for him, but he remained devoted and committed to his first wife, Hannah, never maltreating her.

In chapter one of the verse quoted above, we learn that Elkanah went to Shiloh "with his family", but as time went on, it appeared to be only Hannah going up with her husband to offer the yearly sacrifice. Where was Peninah?

As long as she lived on the face of the earth and in Israel in those days, she must have known how influential Samuel was and how powerfully God was using him. I believe Peninnah must have later been ashamed of the years during which she humiliated Hannah. Whatever happened to Potiphar's wife also?

You may be in a position of influence right now, and all is going well with you. You may have many people serving under you. That's great, but don't forget to keep it real, remain sane, remain under the shadow of the Almighty, and give all the glory to Him. He changes the times and seasons, He resists the proud, and He gives grace to the humble!

"When Pride comes, then comes disgrace, but with the humble is wisdom".

Proverbs 11:2

Questions:

How do I treat people who don't have as much as I do?

Am I fair in my dealings with my employees/subordinates?

DAY TWENTY EIGHT

❖

Diligence At Work.
(Rebecca)

"So she said, "Drink, my lord." Then she quickly let her pitcher down to her hand, and gave him a drink. 19 And when she had finished giving him a drink, she said, "I will draw water for your camels also, until they have finished drinking." 20 Then she quickly emptied her pitcher into the trough, ran back to the well to draw water, *and drew for all his camels".* Genesis 24: 18-20

Rebecca was introduced to us in the Bible as a very industrious and hard-working young woman. Beautiful as she was, she wasn't selling her body. She obviously came from a wealthy home but that didn't stop her from going out to work. How do I know? They had an extra room to lodge guests and camels; she also had a nurse; like a nanny to herself. She had maids, yet she went to fetch water herself.

Trust me when I say that fetching water can be quite tedious! I remember when I was younger; my cousins and I would place plastic buckets on our heads and go fetch water from quite long distances. It was certainly tedious, but Rebecca did it, courteously and joyfully too. Needless to say, destiny met with her while she was at work.

Sometimes, we don't realize we're being watched as we go about our work on a day-to-day basis. Your disposition, charisma, approach, and attitude to work are all being noticed, unknown to you. Recommendations could come from any quarter at any time!

In this age of social media popularity, women must be careful not to get carried away by distractions that affect productivity. Discipline is important in achieving daily tasks and objectives. We must also be careful of the information we put out there about ourselves and families; to a large extent, they tell the kind of people we are. Needless to say that nowadays, recruiters scan through peoples' social media pages to get to know more about them.

"And whatever you do, do it heartily as to the Lord and not to men" Colossians 3:23

Questions?

How Diligent am I at work?

Am I worthy of being recommended?

DAY TWENTY NINE

❖

The Power Of Barter.

Getting What You Want By Exchange (Leah)

"Now Reuben went in the days of wheat harvest and found mandrakes in the field, and brought them to his mother Leah. Then Rachel said to Leah, "Please give me some of your son's mandrakes."

15But she said to her, "Is it a small matter that you have taken away my husband? Would you take away my son's mandrakes also?"

And Rachel said, "Therefore he will lie with you tonight for your son's mandrakes."
Genesis 30: 14-15

Money is a modern means of exchange. However, way before money existed; there was what was called "trade by barter": a means of exchanging what you had for what you wanted. To make money and succeed in today's world, you must have something to offer others in exchange for money: services or products.

Rachael craved mandrakes while Leah wanted alone time with her husband. Leah had somewhat empowered her son with the ability to gather mandrakes and she was then able to use that as a means of exchange, and it worked.

Many women complain about the economy, about how they are not being promoted at work, and how small their salaries are. You can increase your earning capacity by identifying valid ways to meet peoples' needs.

Your diligence will meet with opportunity and you will earn more money.

A friend recently shared with me about an all-women group that organizes "swap parties" in which people bring gently used clothes, shoes, bags, books and household stuffs. The items are expected to be either new or gently used so they can be reusable. During the party, people go to the swap table, present their tally and pick any item they want. By so doing, they get things they need without necessarily spending money; but by exchange. I think it's an amazing idea that can be replicated.

He who has a slack hand becomes poor, but the hand of the diligent makes rich.

Proverbs 10:4

Questions:

What skills or products do I have to offer others in exchange for money?

Can I be relied upon to provide something of value for exchange?

DAY THIRTY

❖

The Power Of Good Works: Raised Back To Life.
(Dorcas)

"There was a believer in Joppa named Tabitha (which in Greek is Dorcas). She
was always doing kind things for others and helping the poor.
39 So Peter returned with them; and as soon as he arrived, they took him to the
upstairs room. The room was filled with widows who were weeping and showing him
the coats and other clothes Dorcas had made for them". Acts 9:36, 39

Some women naturally gravitate toward the needy. There are several
good examples of women who help the cause of the needy through
their NGOs. It's a calling and a career for them. Malala Yousafzai is a
good example of a woman who rose up to stand for a cause, winning
herself a Nobel Prize along the way.

The Nobel Prize is awarded with a monetary gift. Not only does she
find fulfillment in what she does, she has her needs met too.

I read the biography of Madam C. J. Walker recently. She was an
African American entrepreneur and philanthropist. Extolled as the first
female self-made millionaire in America, she became one of the
wealthiest African American women in the country. History has it

recorded that she made her fortune by developing and marketing a line of beauty and hair products for black women, but she was also known for her philanthropy and activism. It is also recorded that she made financial donations to numerous organizations.

Dorcas (from today's scripture) had died, but people were not willing to let her go. Her life had been about helping others. What monetary compensation equals being raised from the dead?

I love to give, and I trust God to help me do so in bigger and more impactful ways!

"We know love by this, that He laid down His life for us; and we ought to lay down our lives for the brethren". I John 3:16

Questions:

Are you a cheerful giver?

Apart from money, what other things do you think you can give to others?

Are you able to defend the cause of the needy?

DAY THIRTY ONE

❖

Having A Competent Custodian.

Working With Trustworthy People (Candace).

"*So he arose and went. And behold, a man of Ethiopia, a eunuch of great authority under Candace the queen of the Ethiopians, who had charge of all her treasury, and had come to Jerusalem to worship*". Acts 8:27

I see a wise tip in this story for women. Candace, the queen of Ethiopia, was very rich. She was most likely a Gentile who didn't know God, but she had appointed someone who was a worshipper of God.

It's one thing to be rich; it's another to be able to manage your wealth. Being wealthy is not about how much you have in your wallet but how your income streams are structured. To remain wealthy, your wealth must keep increasing by means of income-generating sources. As God increases you, the people you place in charge of your finances will be key.

It is imperative to look for trustworthy and faithful people who will manage your business well. You shouldn't try to do everything yourself when God blesses you and you become an owner of many businesses, please delegate, but do so with wisdom and understanding. Whoever it is you place in charge of your finances, always ensure you do your due diligence. Trust but verify, be sure you are on top of whatever it is they are doing for you, by ensuring there are proper lines of accountability and reporting. Run background checks on them and get appropriate references also.

I believe trust must be built over time. Deliberately set people up sometimes and watch out to see if they'll pass the trust test.

Trustworthy messengers refresh like snow in summer.
They revive the spirit of their employer. Proverbs 25:13(NLT)

Questions:

Can I trust those working with and for me?

Do I encourage dishonesty by not putting proper structures in place?

DAY THIRTY TWO

————————— ❖ —————————

Supportive of The Family: The Power of Older Supportive Women.

(Peter's Mother-In-Law)

"Now when Jesus had come into Peter's house, He saw his wife's mother lying sick with a fever. 15So He touched her hand and the fever left her. And she arose and served them".
Matthew 8:14

Here was a woman, living with her daughter and son-in-law. A supportive woman she was; I presume, because not too much was said about her daughter who was Peter's wife .We do know Peter had a wife and a mother-in-law. I like the fact that this elderly woman; the mother in law was on ground to help with the day to day affairs of the family.

She may have developed a fever because she had overworked herself caring for the children or meeting other needs in the house; that we don't know for sure. But we do know that as soon as Jesus healed her, she rose to take care of Him. There was some food available at home; there was provision. She had probably gone to the market in her daughter's absence, and she could cook. She wasn't a mother-in law who was a "terror" in the home.

I love this woman. I see her as a contented person. Why? Peter had left his fishing job, which likely helped him take good care of her daughter, to follow Jesus. Yet, she was still supportive. Some other women would have chastised Peter for not having a paid job, and probably suggested that he was feeding off their daughter.

Grandmothers can also be astute managers, and supportive of their families irrespective of the financial status.

"The older women likewise, that they be reverent in behavior, not slanderers, not given to much wine, teachers of good things— [4] *that they admonish the young women to love their husbands, to love their children".* Titus 2:3-4

Questions:

Am I a good example to the younger generation?

Is my life impactful as a Mother/ a Grandmother/a Mother-in-law?

DAY THIRTY THREE

❖

Savings: In Meeting Up With Life's Demands.

(The Woman With The Issue Of Blood)

"And had suffered many things from many physicians. She had spent all that she had and was no better, but rather grew worse".

Mark 5:26

Mark's narration of this incident indicated the woman must have spent a lot and yet she hadn't been cured. What if she hadn't had anything to spend?

We already discussed the importance of Emergency funds in one of the previous devotionals(Day 10). I talk to women about the importance of having emergency funds and most important; savings all the time. Life can be very uncertain and emergencies could spring up at any time: some unforeseen medical expenses, loss of a breadwinner, loss of a job, or any other cash-depleting situation that could radically alter one's life.

Sure, we pray against evil occurrences but when they do happen, when the righteous fall, they shouldn't remain on the floor; they must get up and keep going!

Every woman must be able to put something aside for herself, and her family, to reduce the effects of emergencies. The family needn't be thrown into despair because there is a need for an emergency surgery.

A good emergency fund will provide the necessary financial cushion.

I have had to rise up to emergencies in my home and rather than borrowing, our emergency savings have always come to the rescue! Like I earlier said, an emergency fund should have enough money for three to six months of one's living expenses.

In this woman's case however, what she spent was much more than Emergency funds; she spent her life savings. Oh she had savings. What if she didn't have any? She would have been neck deep in debts with nobody willing to lend any more to her. She probably might have stopped working. Maybe she even grew anemic because of the constant loss of blood or the regular embarrassment of her dresses being stained by blood. Tough one it must have been!

Savings: A must have! In times of economic recession and famine, there will always be something to fall back to.

"And let them gather all the food of those good years that are coming, and store up grain under the authority of Pharaoh, and let them keep food in the cities. [36] Then that food shall be as a reserve for the land for the seven years of famine which shall be in the land of Egypt, that the land may not perish during the famine."
Genesis 41: 35-36

Questions:

Do you adequately save money for the future or do you eat up all you make?

What can motivate you to develop a saving culture?

DAY THIRTY FOUR

❖

Liberality in the Midst Of Adversity.
The Power Of Hospitality (The Widow Of Zarephath)

"And when he came to the gate of the city, indeed a widow was there gathering sticks. And he called to her and said, "Please bring me a little water in a cup, that I may drink."

11And as she was going to get it, he called to her and said, "Please bring me a morsel of bread in your hand."

12So she said, "As the Lord your God lives, I do not have bread, only a handful of flour in a bin, and a little oil in a jar; and see, I am gathering a couple of sticks that I may go in and prepare it for myself and my son, that we may eat it, and die."

I Kings 17:10-12

Today's devotional is devoted to married and unmarried loving mothers, who are mainly/solely financially responsible for their offspring, either due to the death of a spouse, separation, or divorce.

God had prepared this woman as the one who would feed the prophet Elijah. If anyone had told her in advance about the events and outcome of that day, she probably would have doubted it. God acknowledged the little she had, and so did she. She didn't claim to have nothing.

She wasn't on the side of the road, with her son, begging for alms. She went to gather sticks, still making an effort to survive. She still cared for her son with the little she had and her generosity towards the prophet of God opened the door to unending provision for her family.

God is able to work with the little you have. She even offered Elijah a room in her house! So she had a house too. When she offered the little she had, she entered into a phase of abundance and she was able to offer much more.

"Let nothing be done through selfish ambition or conceit, but in lowliness of mind let each esteem others better than himself.[4] Let each of you look out not only for his own interests, but also for the interests of others". Philippians 2:3-4

Question:

Do you give only out of your abundance or because you can meet a need?

DAY THIRTY FIVE

❖

Sacrificial Giving.
(The Widow Who Gave Her Mite)

"Now Jesus sat opposite the treasury and saw how the people put money into the treasury. And many who were rich put in much. 42Then one poor widow came and threw in two mites, which make a quadrans. 43So He called His disciples to Himself and said to them, "Assuredly, I say to you that this poor widow has put in more than all those who have given to the treasury; 44for they all put in out of their abundance, but she out of her poverty put in all that she had, her whole livelihood."

Mark 12: 44

On this fateful day, Jesus sat at the treasury observing how the people gave their offerings. This indicates to us that He is interested in what we give to God as offerings. Many people say churches extort their members when it comes to giving offerings, but the truth is, God does expect us to give of our substance to Him. Sure, size does not matter but it does also matter in relation to what you have. The woman had so little but Jesus felt her offering was sacrificial than the big offerings some other people brought.

I have learnt over time that offerings open up the door to God's blessings in our lives. Tithes belong to God; you are merely returning His money to Him when you pay them. Offerings, however, are your freewill gifts to Him!

84

A few years ago, I realized that the size of my offerings had remained relatively the same for a few years. What! No one wants God's blessings over their lives to remain at the same level for years. Never! I endeavour to increase my offering from time to time; especially at the beginning of each new year.

"So let each one give as he purposes in his heart, not grudgingly or of necessity; for God loves a cheerful giver". II Cor 9:7

Questions:

Do I give cheerfully or grudgingly?

DAY THIRTY SIX

❖

Multiple Sources Of Income: Hardwork And Hospitality (Rahab)

"(But she had brought them up to the roof and hidden them with the stalks of flax, which she had laid in order on the roof.)" Joshua 2:6.

Again, we look at the life of another woman who had a couple of different things to do. Rahab; humanly imperfect, but a perfect tool in the hands of God. One thing that gets me thinking concerning Rahab's life is the reason why she went into prostitution.

Joshua 2:6 says she had flax in her house, which she used to hide the two spies from Israel. Flax is a food and fiber crop grown in cooler parts of the world, according to wikipedia.org. From flax, you can get food, textiles, (linen in particular), and oil. So I believe she must have been rich and financially comfortable; she must have had a flourishing business.

She had her own house, located on the city wall, in fact. So I believe she wasn't into prostitution for money. Was it for loneliness? She had probably been through some tough challenges in life, her self-esteem may have been damaged, and she desired an inner satisfaction that she just couldn't seem to find. Just like the woman by the well, she may have thought being promiscuous would satisfy her inner cravings.

Most of the time, prostitutes "conduct business with their clients" in hidden places, but she openly set her own business on the top of the wall, and visible for all to see.....hmm. She must have been a meticulous woman, seeing that she had laid the flax in order. She was also a well-known woman in the society, because the king knew her and sent a word to her when the spies came to her house.

God recognizes hardwork and diligence too. It's not just about spirituality or how much of the Word we can quote. Principles come to play in life. Well-rounded people are useful in God's hands. Where would she have hidden the spies if she hadn't had a spare room or flax or a house. She was single but fulfilled, and had multiple streams of income in addition.

She might have been a prostitute by profession, but she was also hospitable and had a good heart. This woman enjoyed the mercy of God, and God's mercy is truly all we need. He can choose to lift anyone He wants. That's God for you. And so He chose this woman. Having said all that; no one can continue in sin and expect God's grace to abound. Remain diligent in what is good and acceptable; your opportunity to be shown to the world is just around the corner!

"Give, and it will be given to you: good measure, pressed down, shaken together, and running over will be put into your bosom. For with the same measure that you use, it will be measured back to you." Luke 6:38

Questions:

What are those things that constantly hinder me from becoming my best and optimally using my talents in life? Do you have any hidden talents that can be harnessed?

DAY THIRTY SEVEN

❖

Multi-giftedness, Versatility and Courage
(Deborah)

"Now Deborah, a prophetess, the wife of Lapidoth, was judging Israel at that time.
5 And she would sit under the palm tree of Deborah between Ramah and Bethel in
the mountains of Ephraim. And the children of Israel came up to her for judgment".
Judges 5:4

Deborah is a typical example of a multi-gifted woman who didn't allow
the circumstances of the economy to restrict or limit her. It was said
that in her times, village life had ceased, the highways were deserted
and everything looked gloomy. She drew strength from within to be
what and who God wanted her to be. Quite a lot of people are multi-
faceted and gifted to do a lot of things. Many of us are blessed with
more than one, two, or even five talents. When we use our gifts, we can
then enjoy the blessings associated with them!

Deborah was a prophetess, and she may have enjoyed prophet offerings
and other gifts from time to time. She was a judge; she may have received
token payments for passing judgments. She was also a Mother-in Israel;
even if she hasn't been paid in cash, she must have been paid in kind. She
was so respected that the King couldn't go to war without her.

She followed the king to war and they got the victory! If the king did not give her monetary and other gifts, he must have conferred on her the title of an OON (Officer of the Order of the Niger) or OBE (The Order of the British Empire) -that alone would have been huge reward for her labor!

What can you do? Put your gifts to work! Let them find expression; don't hold back. Live maximally!

"Who through faith subdued kingdoms, worked righteousness, obtained promises, stopped the mouths of lions,[34] quenched the violence of fire, escaped the edge of the sword, out of weakness were made strong, became valiant in battle, turned to flight the armies of the aliens". Hebrews 11:34

Question:

The economy looks bleak, nonetheless, which of my potentials can impact my generation?

DAY THIRTY EIGHT

❖

Making Wise Investment Choices.
(Pharaoh's Daughter)

"And Pharaoh's daughter said to her, "Go." So the maiden went and called the child's mother. 9Then Pharaoh's daughter said to her, "Take this child away and nurse him for me, and I will give you your wages." So the woman took the child and nursed him. 10And the child grew, and she brought him to Pharaoh's daughter, and he became her son. So she called his name Moses, saying, "Because I drew him out of the water". Exodus 2:8-10

Many times are we confronted with risky investments and we reject them out of fear and uncertainty. Remember that we may never have heard of this unnamed daughter of Pharaoh if not for her singular act of rescuing Moses from death. Well, she never thought of what she would gain in return by rescuing Moses out of water; it was an act of help which rather turned out as a worthy investment.

She invested her money to hire Jochebed as the nanny she supposed she was. When Moses was older, he was brought to the palace, where Pharaoh's daughter then invested her time raising him up as her own son.

More often than not, the best of opportunities do not come in shiny packages. When we allow the Holy Spirit to inspire us, we can see those opportunities, take giant steps, and embark on journeys that will change lives for eternity.

Pharaoh's daughter's act was instrumental in Moses' life. Her investment turned out to be a fantastic one! Moses became an instrument in God's hands, a deliverer of His people and her act of saving him from the water was recorded in the bible; even though she was unnamed.

"Send your grain across the seas, and in time, profits will flow back to you. But divide your investments among many places for you do not know what risks might lie ahead". Ecclesiastes 11:1-2(NLT)

Questions:

Are there things and people I can invest in?

Are there people around me I can help to

achieve some of their potentials?

DAY THIRTY NINE

❖

Protecting Our Children By All Means.

First Things First :(The Unnamed Woman In II Kings 6)

"Then, as the king of Israel was passing by on the wall, a woman cried out to him, saying, "Help, my lord, O king!"27And he said, "If the Lord does not help you, where can I find help for you? From the threshing floor or from the winepress?" 28Then the king said to her, "What is troubling you?"And she answered, "This woman said to me, 'Give your son, that we may eat him today, and we will eat my son tomorrow.' 29So we boiled my son, and ate him. And I said to her on the next day, 'Give your son, that we may eat him'; but she has hidden her son."

II Kings 6:26-29

The story in the scripture above is a rather sad one. May we never experience times of drought like these women did. It was so bad that they resorted to cannibalism; devouring one of their children, for that matter!

For this story to have been included in the Bible there must be a lesson to learn from it.

These women needed food, by all means, for their survival. They had expended their emergency funds and other savings. Their husbands may have deserted them, out of shame or in an attempt to go searching for food. Their final resolve was to kill their sons for food. Of course, one of them knew she wasn't truly going to do that but, unfortunately, the other was so gullible to have done so. Whose interest should she have protected more? Hers or her son's? Sadly, the woman who suggested the wicked idea was the one who hid her own son after devouring the other woman's son. That also teaches us to be wary of ideas coming from people, especially when they are not in line with the word of God. Does it ever sound right to indulge in cannibalism? Talk less of devouring your own son. What a wicked world!

All families face tough times, but even in the midst of such; we must endeavor to place our children's best interests above ours (especially when they are young and vulnerable) and trust God to meet all our needs. I am convinced the other woman's son wasn't killed eventually, because just a few days or even hours later, the drought situation turned around for good. But by then, the woman who lived for the moment had already lost her son!

Whose needs come first: yours or your immediate family's?

"Children are a gift from the Lord; they are a reward from him.
4 Children born to a young man; are like arrows in a warrior's hands.
5 How joyful is the man whose quiver is full of them! He will not be put to shame when
he confronts his accusers at the city gates". Psalm 127:3-5

Questions:

Am I faithfully mothering my children in partnership with God or am I allowing the distractions and pressures of the world get in the way?

DAY FORTY

❖

The Woman Reading This Book.

Your name may not have been written in the Bible and you may not have lived in Bible times; nevertheless, you matter in God's agenda and your story is a beautiful one that will be read by generations to come!

"You made all the delicate, inner parts of my body, and knit me together in my mother's womb.[14] Thank you for making me so wonderfully complex! Your workmanship is marvelous—how well I know it". Psalm 139:13-14

Questions:

What are your life and financial goals?

What things have you learnt in this devotional and plan to put into practice, starting now?

Where do you see yourself in five years time, with regards to managing your God-given resources?

What story would you want written about you?

Now, go ahead and write your story the way you want it read!

God bless you!

OTHER BOOKS BY THE AUTHOR

❖

God's Choice of the Chosen
(7 Vs' about David) **(Co-Authored)**

"God's Choice of the Chosen"
is an expository book that explores the life and lessons of an
extraordinary Bible character called David.

Pebbles From The Rock

"Pebbles from the Rock"
is a 70-day compilation of inspired thoughts.
They address the day-to-day needs of everybody vis-à-vis the
experiences of Bible characters.

NOTE FROM THE AUTHOR

— ❖ —

Thank you for reading this book.

I believe you have been blessed.

Please help spread the word to every woman who desires
to have an amazing financial life.

You may purchase this book as a gift for someone;

You may recommend it within your circles for joint study
purposes.

Read, Review and Recommend

Thank you.

TO CONTACT THE AUTHOR

❖

For more information about the author; Sola Adesakin,

special discounts about this Book and all other inquiries,

Please email:

info@fruitfoundation.org

info@smartstewards.com

Or Visit:

www.fruitfoundation.org

www.smartstewards.com

www.ingramcontent.com/pod-product-compliance
Lightning Source LLC
Chambersburg PA
CBHW051816040426
42446CB00007B/702